Copyright © 2019 by T. Irvolino
All rights reserved. No part of this book may be used or reproduced or transmitted in any form or by any means, electronic or mechanical including photocopying, recording, or by any information storage or retrieval system without express written permission from the publisher.

The information provided within this Book is for general informational purposes only. While we try to keep the information up-to-date and correct, there are no representations or warranties, express or implied, about the completeness, accuracy, reliability, suitability or availability with respect to the information, products, services, or related graphics contained in this Book for any purpose. Any use of this information is at your own risk.

The methods describe within this Book are the author's personal thoughts. They are not intended to be a definitive set of instructions for this project. You may discover there are other methods and materials to accomplish the same end result.

The author has made every effort to ensure the accuracy of the information within this book was correct at time of publication. The author and publisher do not assume and hereby disclaims any liability to any party for any loss, damage, or disruption caused by errors or omissions, whether such errors or omissions result from accident, negligence, or any other cause.

Sun Media Group, LLC
First Book Publication Date: 4/2019
Cover Illustration: T. Irvolino
To contact Author, please email publisher: sunmediagroupllc@gmail.com

KISS MY A**
I'M COLORING BITCHES

Kiss My A** I'm Coloring Bitches is perfect to way to say the things you really want to say! I couldn't stop laughing as I was creating it for you. Sit back, relax and color your words, don't say em.

CONTAINS ADULT LANGUAGE. NOT INTENDED FOR CHILDREN.

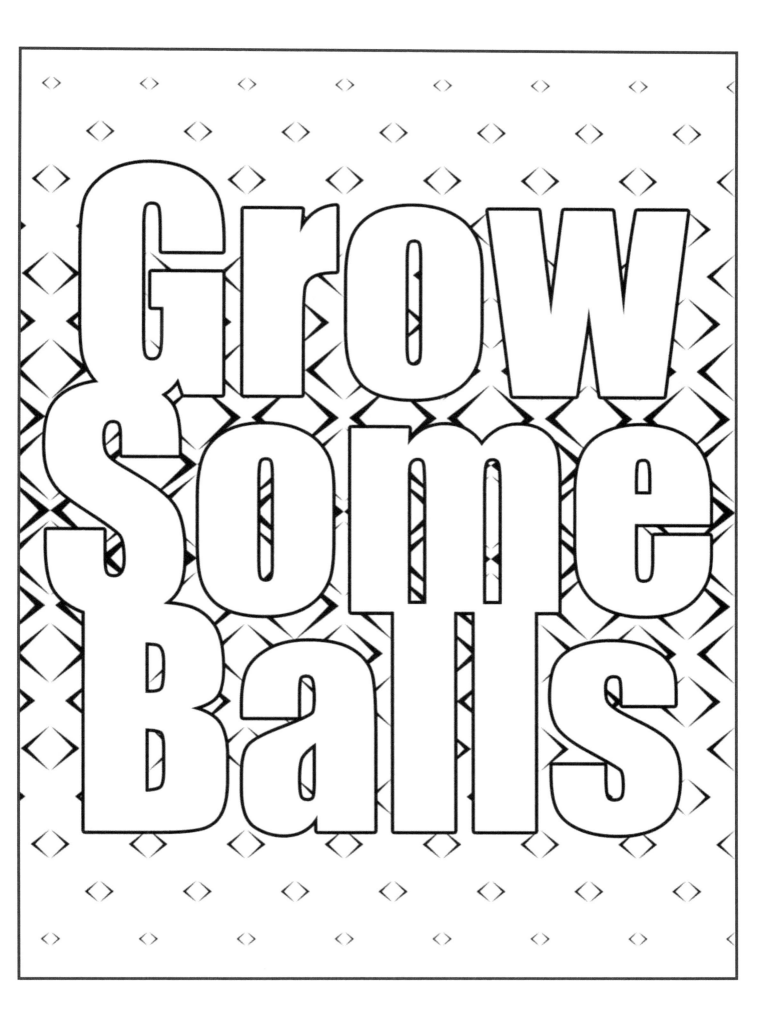

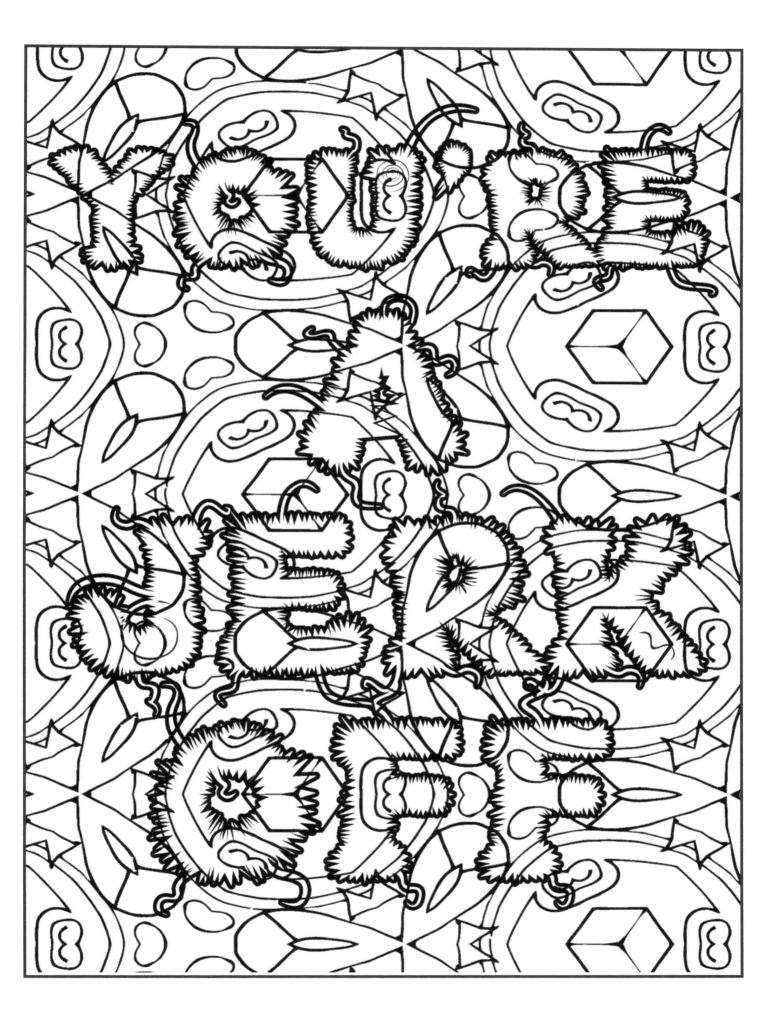

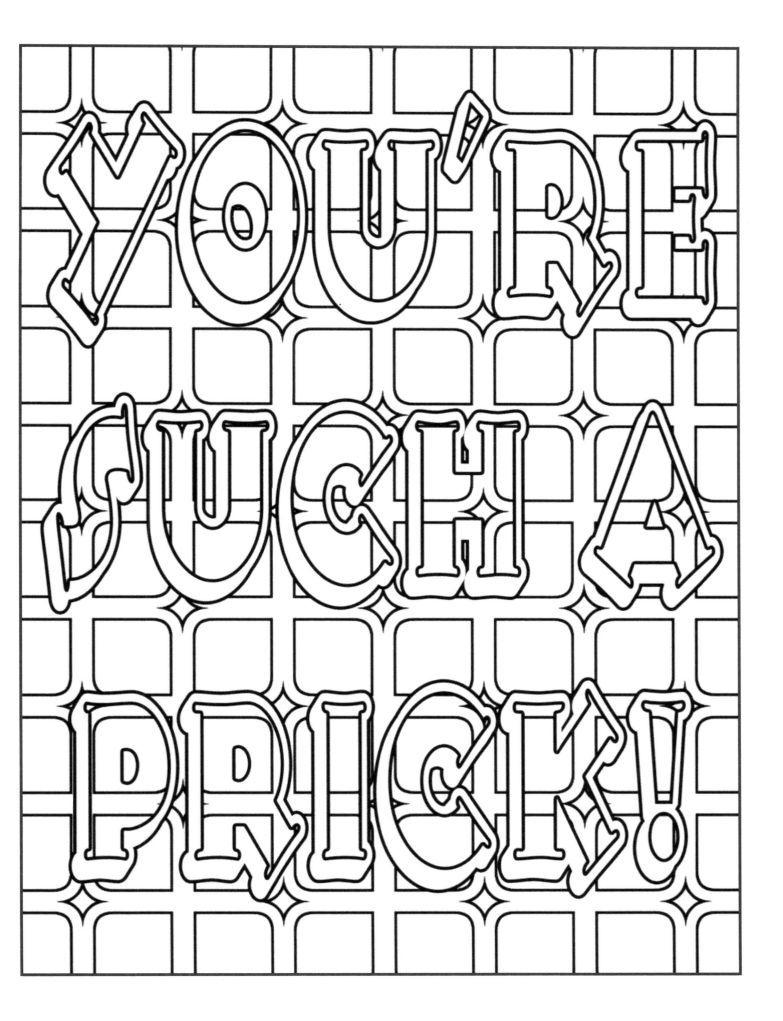

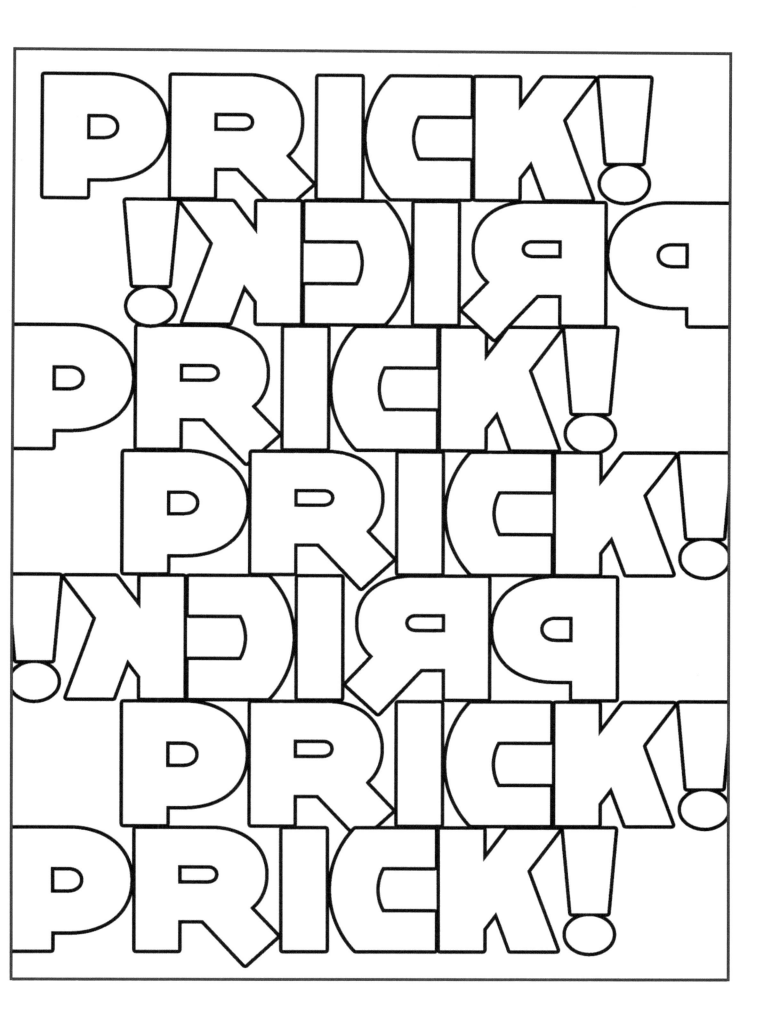

Thank you for choosing my coloring book. I really hope you'll enjoy hours of stress-free coloring and laughs. There are plenty of books out there that are similar to us, but we're ecstatic that you've decided to choose us. I'd love to hear your thoughts once you've got your hands on it!

Thank you for your support!

CPSIA information can be obtained
at www.ICGtesting.com
Printed in the USA
LVHW022137260623
750878LV00036B/839